Chilu Baby
and other stories

Illustrated by Rahul Deshpande

JYOTSNA PRAKASHAN

Chilu Baby : JP 258

Published by :
Milind L. Paranjape
Jyotsna Prakashan
'Dhavalgiri',
430-31 Shaniwar Peth
Pune 411030

Mumbai Office :
Mohan Building,
162 J. Shankarsheth Marg
Girgaum, Mumbai 400004

First Edition : March 2011
Reprint : 2016

Printed by : Unique Offset
Narhegaon, Pune 411041

Price Rs 70/-

ISBN 978-81-7925-276-5

Chilu Baby

There was a squirrel. She had one baby. His name was Chilu. He was a very happy baby.

It was summer. Chilu Baby was playing outside. Suddenly the sky got cloudy.

Soon it started to rain. Chilu Baby was delighted. He began to jump up and down happily. But the rain did not last long. It fell for a while and then stopped. Chilu felt bad.

His mother said, “It was a shower. Maybe it will rain again tomorrow.”

The next day Chilu Baby sat waiting for rain. But the rain didn’t come. Then Chilu went to his mother. He said, “Mama, Mama, I want rain.”

His mother tried to tell him he must wait for a few days. But he was stubborn. “I want rain right now.” Chilu Baby would not eat or drink anything.

Just then a parrot came. He said, “I’ll give you a nice, sweet guava.”

Chilu Baby said, “I don’t want a guava. I want RAIN right now!”

After a while a peacock came. He said, “I’ll show you a pretty dance.”

Chilu Baby said, “I don’t want to see a dance. I want RAIN!”

Then a kite came. She said, “Come, I’ll take you for a ride high in the sky.”

But Chilu Baby wanted rain. He wouldn’t stop crying.

Then came an elephant. The elephant asked, “What is the matter?”

Chilu Baby said, “I want rain right now.”

The elephant said, “Is that all? Wait a moment.”

The elephant went to the lake nearby. He took some of the water in his trunk and went back to Chilu Baby. Then he sprayed the water all over him.

Chilu Baby was overjoyed. He began to dance.
"It's raining, it's raining!"

The Tiger's Beard

There was a big jungle. In it there lived a tiger. He would hunt deer, and after eating he would feel sleepy. Nearby there was a small temple, where he would go and sit yawning and dozing.

One day as he was dozing off like this, he saw a goat. The goat had a nice beard. The tiger thought, 'Because of his beard how fine the goat looks! But here I am, the king of the jungle, and still I don't have a beard. If I had a beard how grand I would look. I have a beautiful colour and jet black stripes. But why don't I have a beard? I want a beard.' The tiger felt bad, and began to cry.

What could he do? He started to think.

Then he went into the temple. He said to the god, "Give me a beard."

Then little by little a beard began to grow. He ran his hand over it. He was happy. With a big smile he said to himself, 'Now I am going to look grand.' He said to the God, "God, make my beard longer." Little by little his beard grew long.

Suddenly he had a thought, now I must go hunting. He got up and started to walk. But his beard got underfoot. No matter how he stepped, the beard came in his way. He began to run, but again the beard came underfoot. Then he got angry with the beard. Finally he managed to crawl near a pool of water and drink. But as he drank, the hair of his beard came into his mouth. He began to cry. He said to the God, "God, I don't want a beard. I'm hungry and thirsty. Take the beard back."

The God said to him, "You were so beautiful! Are you again going to look at somebody else and ask for what he has?"

The tiger answered, "No. no. Never again." Then he lost his beard and was happy as he had been before.

The Hardworking Hen

Once there was a hen. She had two friends, Brother Duck and Brother Rabbit. Once as she was walking around, she found some grains of wheat. She thought, "I'll plant this seed." Then she said, "Brother Duck, Brother Rabbit, let's plant the seed. . ."

They both said, "We want to go and play right now."

So the hen dug a little hole and planted the seed in that.

Then she said, "Brother Duck, Brother Rabbit, come. Let's water. . . ."

Both of them yawned and said, "We want to go to sleep right now."

So the hen watered the plant by herself.

Slowly the seeds sprouted. The seedlings started to grow.

The hen said, “Brother Duck, Brother Rabbit, now let’s spread some manure. . . .”

But they both said, “We want to play ball now.”

So the hen spread the manure by herself.

Slowly the seedlings grew taller and the grain ripened.

The hen said, "Brother Duck, Brother Rabbit, let's cut the wheat. . . ."

They said, "We can't come. We want to go for a walk."

So the hen cut the wheat by herself.

After she cut the wheat she said, "Brother Duck, Brother Rabbit, let's grind the wheat."

They said, "We can't come. We don't feel like doing anything!"

So the hen ground the wheat by herself.

Then she said, “Brother Duck, Brother Rabbit, let’s make chapaties.”

They said, “Why do you keep bothering us? Go and make the chapaties yourself.”

The poor hen rolled the chapaties and cooked them herself.

Smelling the cooking chapaties, the duck and the rabbit peeped into the kitchen.

They said, "Sister Hen, Sister Hen, give us some chapaties to eat."

The hen said, "So now you come to eat, when everything is ready! But you didn't want to do any work! I'm not going to give you any chapaties."

Then the duck and the rabbit realized their mistake. They begged her pardon. And then the three of them sat together and ate the nice hot chapaties.

The Long-Eared Fellow

There was a rabbit.
He was very hungry.
He went looking for
something to eat.
Finally he found a pond.
That made him
very happy.

He ran to the
pond. He ate the
grass on the bank.
There were some carrots
there, and he ate them too.
He drank the nice cool water
of the pond. Then he began to yawn.
He went to a nearby cave and fell asleep.

It was the cave of a tiger. After a while the tiger came back. He heard someone snoring inside.

The tiger asked, “Who has entered my cave?”

The rabbit answered,

> “It’s me, it’s me, the long-eared fellow,
> I’m doze doze dozing, don’t come near me!
> I’ll smash the eyes of Brother Tiger!”

Hearing this, the tiger ran away in fright.

On the way he met a lion. The lion asked him, "Hey, what happened? Are you frightened of something?"

The tiger said, "What can I say? Somebody has entered my cave and is saying he will smash my eyes!"

The lion said, "Is that so? Come on, let's have a look."

Then with the lion in the lead, followed by the tiger they went to the cave.

The lion asked, "Who has entered the tiger's cave?"

The rabbit said,

> "It's me, it's me, the long-eared fellow,
> I'm doze doze dozing, don't come near me!
> I'll smash the eyes of Brother Tiger!
> I'll grab the mane of Brother Lion!"

The lion was also frightened. He said, "Let's get out of here my friend. He'll grab my mane! Come quick!"

Both ran away.

On the way they met an elephant.

The elephant asked, "Hey, what happened? Why are you both running in fright?"

The lion said, "What can we say? Somebody has entered the tiger's cave, and he says he'll grab my mane, and smash the tiger's eyes."

The elephant said, “Come on, let’s have a look. I’ll come with you.”

Then with the elephant in the lead, followed by the lion and the tiger, the three of them went to the cave.

The elephant asked, “Who has entered the tiger’s cave?”

The rabbit said,

“It’s me, it’s me, the long-eared fellow,
I’m doze doze dozing, don’t come near me!
I’ll smash the eyes of Brother Tiger!
I’ll grab the mane of Brother Lion!
I’ll cut off Brother Elephant’s trunk!”

Hearing this, the elephant was also frightened. The three of them went running.

On the way they met Sister Bear.

She asked, “What’s the matter? What are you running away from?”

The elephant answered, “Sister Bear, what can we say? Somebody has entered the tiger’s cave. He says he will cut off my trunk, grab the lion’s mane, and smash the tiger’s eyes.”

The bear said, "Come on, let's have a look."

Then with the bear in the lead, followed by the elephant, the lion and last of all the tiger, they all went to the cave.

The bear asked, "Who has entered the tiger's cave?"

The rabbit answered from inside,

"It's me, it's me, the long-eared fellow,
I'm doze doze dozing, don't come near me!
I'll smash the eyes of Brother Tiger!
I'll grab the mane of Brother Lion!
I'll cut off Brother Elephant's trunk!
I'll pull the hair of Sister Bear!"

Hearing this, the bear said in fright, "Oh my! He says he will pull my hair."

They all started running. On the way they met a fox. He asked, "Why are you running in fright? What happened?"

Then Sister Bear said, "Someone has entered the tiger's cave, and he says he'll pull my hair, cut off the elephant's trunk, grab the lion's mane, and smash the tiger's eyes."

The fox said, "Come on then. Let's have a look. I'll go first."

Then the fox, followed by Sister Bear, then the elephant, the lion and the tiger, all went to the cave.

The fox was clever. He stood outside the cave and asked in a loud voice, "Who has entered the tiger's cave?"

Then the rabbit answered from inside,

> "It's me, it's me, the long-eared fellow.
> I'm doze doze dozing, don't come near me!
> I'll smash the eyes of Brother Tiger,
> I'll grab the mane of Brother Lion,
> I'll cut off Brother Elephant's trunk,
> I'll pull the hair of Sister Bear,
> I'll pull the tail of Brother Fox!"

The fox answered, "I'll pull your ears, my little friend!"

The rabbit said to himself, 'Oh my! It looks like he knows who I am!'

And he shot out from the back door of the cave.

Then the fox said to all of them, "Why, it's just a little rabbit! And you were afraid of him?"

Nannytai

There once was a Nanny-goat. She had two kids. On summer days they suffered from the sun, in the rainy season from the rain, and in the winter from the cold. So Nanny-goat decided to build a house for her kids. She said to the kids, "Children, you sit under the tree. I'm going to get material for our house."

Nearby there was a big tar road. A bullock cart with sugarcane was coming down the road. Nanny-goat went and stopped in front of the cart.

The driver said, "Hey, Nanny, get out of the way!"

Nanny-goat said, "Don't call me Nanny. Call me Nannytai."

The driver said, "Nannytai, please move out of the way!"

Then Nannytai said to the driver, "I'm building a house. Will you give me some stalks of sugarcane?"

The driver gave her some stalks of cane.

Then Nannytai went back to her kids, singing,

Cane for the pillars, cane for the pillars,
Let's build a house!

She set up the sugarcane pillars. Then she went out on the road again. A bullock cart with grass was coming. She spoke to the driver very politely, "I'm building a house. Will you give me some grass?"

The driver gave her armful of grass. She then again went back to her kids, singing,

Cane for the pillars, grass for the walls,
Let's build a house!

Then she made the walls of grass and also made a little door.

When she went out on the road again she saw an old lady walking on the road with a stick in her hand. The old lady had a bundle on her head. Nannytai asked her, "Granny, what do you have in your bundle?" The old lady said, "Nannytai, I would give you some, but you wouldn't be able to chew them."

"What is it in your bundle?"

The old lady said, "Dates, dried dates!"

Nannytai said, "I'm building a house, so would you please give me some dates?"

The old lady replied, "Yes, I'll give you some, but help me put the bundle down."

The old lady gave Nannytai a handful of dates. Nannytai took the dates and went back to her kids.

> Cane for the pillars, grass for the walls, dates for the tiles,
> Let's build a house!

Nannytai tiled the roof of the dates. Her lovely house was ready. She seated the kids inside and said to them, "I'm going out for a while. You stay inside and close the door. Don't open it up for anyone. When I come I'll say, 'Cane for the pillars, grass for the walls, dates for the tiles, Open the door!' Only then should you open the door."

There was a tiger hiding nearby. He was listening to everything.

When he saw Nannytai had gone, he went to the house and began to sing,

> Cane for the pillars, grass for the walls, dates for the tiles,
> Open the door!

The kids carefully looked through a crack in the door. Then they whispered softly, "It's the tiger!" They kept completely still, not making a single sound. The tiger angrily sang the song once more,

> Cane for the pillars, grass for the walls, dates for the tiles,
> Open the door!

The kids didn't make a sound. They kept completely still. Finally the tiger stamped off. In a little while Nannytai came back. She called,

> Cane for the pillars, grass for the walls, dates for the tiles,
> Open the door!

The kids knew it was their mother's voice. They peeped through the crack, "Mother's come, Mother's come!" They opened the door and said, "Mother, Mother, the tiger came but we didn't open the door!" Then Nannytai said, "How clever my children are!" And she held them close.